WAYLAND
www.waylandbooks.co.uk

Contents

Fire!
PREVENT IT

Fire! Fire!

For thousands of years people have used fire to cook food and to keep warm. It is used in all sorts of ways in industry too, such as heating iron to make steel. There's no doubt about it, fire is a very useful thing. But it can also be very dangerous ...

STEEL MANUFACTURING IN THE UNITED KINGDOM

Using fire in industry: a steel-making plant in Sheffield, UK

Throughout history, fire has been a danger to people – so there are many ways it has been fought. This book will tell the story of how firefighting has changed over time, look at some of the equipment that has been used and train you to think carefully about fire safety.

Fire spreads quickly, burning everything and anything in its path. More people die in fires by inhaling smoke than through burns.

Smoke contains all sorts of dangerous chemicals. When we inhale smoke, it fills our lungs making it difficult for us to breathe. Around seven out of every ten deaths caused by fire are the result of inhaling smoke.

FIRE SAFETY

Fire can break out anywhere, so it's important to know what to do. Turn to page 30 for action steps!

Roman firefighters

Historians believe that the very first fire brigade was formed in Rome in 6 CE. Roman firefighters were called vigiles, which means 'watchmen'. The Rome fire service had five hundred men.

When the Romans invaded Britain in 43 CE, they brought brigades of vigiles with them. This was Britain's first organised fire service. When the Romans left, the vigiles left, too. Britain would have to wait more than 1,200 years before it got another fire service.

The Great Fire of Rome

In 64 CE, Rome was engulfed by a terrible fire. The vigiles did their best, but they were overwhelmed by the ferocity of the blaze. This is how one Roman historian, Tacitus, described it:

Everybody was shrieking and crying. Nothing could be seen clearly for the smoke. A wind arose and spread the flames over the whole city. The people crowded to the countryside and lay in the fields.

This is the entrance to one of the vigiles barracks. When it was discovered in 1865, it was covered in Roman graffiti. These inscriptions revealed the motto of the fire service: Ubi Dolor Ibi Vigiles, which means, "Where there is grief, there are firemen".

The Great Fire of Rome lasted a whole week, by which time the once-great city had been reduced to a smouldering pile of rubble and ashes. At the time, many Romans blamed their unpopular Emperor, Nero, for starting the fire. However, this is unlikely since the Emperor was staying on the coast, miles away from Rome, at the time.

The Great Fire of London

By the late 1600s there were still no organised fire services in Britain. Then, on the night of Sunday 2nd September 1666, there occurred an event that changed attitudes to firefighting forever.

This tax return lists 'Thomas Farrinor, Baker' – his oven is believed to have started the fire

Fire broke out in a small bakery in Pudding Lane, near London Bridge. It probably started when a pile of logs was set alight by a spark from the baker's oven.

The houses in London were made of wood, and because the weather had been warm and dry, the timber burned very quickly. A strong wind blew the blaze from one building to another. People filled leather buckets with water to try and put the fire out, but soon the whole of the City of London was engulfed in flames. Buildings were pulled down to create a firebreak, a wide gap across which it was hoped the flames wouldn't be able to spread.

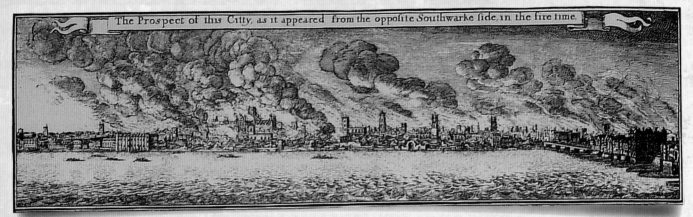

The Prospect of this Citty, as it appeared from the opposite Southwarke side, in the fire time.

By the time the fire was put out three days later, it had destroyed over 13,000 homes and 84 churches, including St Paul's Cathedral. Unsurprisingly, it become known as the Great Fire of London.

A monument was built to commemorate the Great Fire of London, which can still be seen today. It is 62 metres high and is the tallest freestanding stone column in the world.

As the City of London began to be rebuilt, people started to think about ways in which they could protect their new homes against fire. It wasn't long before some enterprising businesses popped up!

The Monument to the Great Fire of London

Fire marks and fire men

As a way of trying to prevent another fire like the Great Fire of London, businesspeople started up what they called 'fire insurance' companies.

The fire insurance companies quickly realised that if a fire was put out quickly, the building wouldn't suffer too much damage and they wouldn't have to pay to rebuild it. So they began to employ small teams of men who could run to the location of a fire and try to put it out quickly. It didn't take long for people to start calling these teams 'fire men'.

Seventeenth-century fire men at work

Only rich people could afford to insure their houses. If you were poor and your house caught fire, there was no one to help – you had to try and put it out yourself with any buckets and water you could find.

A metal plate, called a 'fire mark', was put up on the front of your house to show which insurance company you were with.

Can you spot the fire mark on this old house?

Clue: it's above one of the bedroom windows:

The father of the modern fire service

The fire insurance companies went from strength to strength, but their firefighters still only went to buildings which were insured. However, in 1824 things began to change. The world's very first public fire service, run by a local council, was formed in the city of Edinburgh.

The man chosen by Edinburgh Council to run the city's fire service was James Braidwood. His job title was Master of Fire Engines. James Braidwood believed that a good fire service needed good firefighters. He made sure that the members of his team were all healthy, fit and properly trained. Crucially, he also wrote a book outlining his ideas, so his methods were put into practice in towns and cities all over Britain.

James Braidwood

The Tooley Street Fire

In 1833, aged just 33, James Braidwood moved to London and ran the new London Fire Engine Establishment for the next 28 years. On 22nd June 1861, a fire broke out at some warehouses in Tooley Street near London Bridge station. When Braidwood arrived at the fire, he found that it was out of control. He discovered that the fire doors had been left open, allowing the fire to spread. As he stepped inside the warehouse to investigate further, the front of the building collapsed on top of him. He was killed instantly.

In 2008, a memorial to James Braidwood was unveiled in Edinburgh. It reads:
James Braidwood
1800–1861
Father of the British Fire Service.

Deane's smoke helmet

The Tooley Street Fire was thought to have been the worst fire in London since the Great Fire of 1666. But developments in technology during the nineteenth century meant that fire safety was improving, particularly when it came to the dangers of smoke.

Charles Deane invented the 'smoke helmet' in the 1800s. Having worked in the London dockyards, he had seen for himself the hazards of fighting fires in the holds of ships.

Deane's smoke helmet was made of copper and weighed about 14 kg. A long leather hose at the back of the helmet was used to supply air to the firefighter.

Deane's smoke helmet looks like something a medieval knight might have worn – that's where he got his idea from. His brother John was visiting a big country house when a fire broke out in the stables. John put on the helmet from a suit of armour that was on display. Firefighters fed him air through the helmet using their hoses and he managed to rescue all of the horses.

Firefighters today use 'breathing apparatus sets' to protect them against smoke or chemical fumes. This is simply a modern version of Deane's smoke helmet, since it consists of cylinders of air connected by a tube to a face mask. Each cylinder of air lasts for thirty to thirty-five minutes.

The steam pump

In 1829, John Braithwaite invented a new kind of machine that would change firefighting forever. It was the world's first ever steam pump.

Before the steam pump was invented, firefighters had to pump water by hand, using 'stirrup pumps'. This was very hard work – worse still, the water came out of stirrup pumps at such a slow rate that it would often freeze solid in winter! John Braithwaite's steam fire pump could pump over 650 litres of water a minute; there was no way that water gushing out of a hose at that speed would freeze.

A company called Merryweathers became one of the main manufacturers of steam pumps. To remind their customers just how good their machines were at pumping out lots of water very fast, they gave them names like 'Torrent' and 'Deluge'.

An 1862 Merryweather Steam Pump

Some items of firefighting equipment, like ladders, hoses and, of course, axes, haven't changed much since Roman times. When firefighters retire, they are often presented with a special axe.

Using the massive power of its engine, a modern firefighting vehicle like this one can pump water through a hose at the rate of around 4,500 litres a minute

The modern fire engine

In the nineteenth century, horses were usually used to pull steam pumps, which was a slow process. Luckily, a brand new invention arrived that made getting to fires a whole lot quicker.

The first petrol-engine motor car appeared on British roads in 1894. Seven years later, in 1901, the town of Eccles in Lancashire boasted the country's first motorised fire engine. Compared to the fire trucks of today, it wasn't very good. It could only carry five firefighters and didn't have room for any water tanks. Its top speed was 22 km/h!

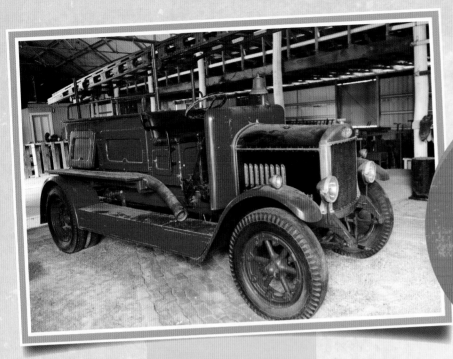

A Dennis N Type Fire Engine from the early twentieth century

Dennis Specialist Vehicles built their first fire engine in 1907. The company is still building fire engines today.

In the 1920s, 'specialist' motorised fire engines began to appear, like those that had a large, extending ladder so that firefighters could get to the top of tall buildings.

Over the years, motorised fire engines got faster and larger, so that they could carry large tanks of water, as well as ladders, hoses and plenty of firefighters.

A modern fire service has a variety of vehicles, which might include an off-roader, a large lorry with heavy lifting gear and a command unit with radio and IT systems for major incidents.

Britain's first women firefighters

Until the twentieth century, there weren't many women firefighters. It was thought that they weren't fit enough and that it was an improper job for ladies. There were some exceptions, though!

Girton College Fire Brigade

In 1878, the students of Girton College, a women's college near Cambridge, were appalled by the damage caused by a fire in a field at a neighbouring farm. They decided they needed to create a volunteer fire brigade.

They asked the Superintendent of the Metropolitan Fire Brigade in London, Captain Eyre Massey Shaw, for his support. But Captain Shaw didn't believe it was a woman's job to be a firefighter and refused to give them any help at all.

So the women of Girton College started their own fire brigade. They learnt how to use escape ladders, hoses, pumps and axes. They even dug a pond in the college grounds to provide water for firefighting. The pond is still there; it's part of the College's wildlife garden.

At the beginning of the twentieth century, people became more aware of the danger of fires in the workplace. Shops and factories started to form their own company fire brigades. These fire brigades were made up of people who worked for the shop or factory, both men and women.

These days there are many women working as firefighters. The first woman to become a full-time professional firefighter in the UK was Sue Batten, who joined the London Fire Brigade in 1982.

Women firefighters are a common sight today

19

The growth of local fire brigades

At the beginning of the twentieth century, every town in Britain wanted to be like the big cities and have its very own fire brigade. By 1938, there were around 1,500 town brigades around the country, all of them different.

As well as attending fires at people's homes, local fire brigades were responsible for fighting fires in public places. In 1929, the Paisley Fire Brigade attended a fire at the town's Glen Cinema, where 69 children died because the fire doors were locked. This and other tragedies shocked the nation, and Parliament passed new laws requiring cinemas and theatres to have proper fire exits that opened outwards and had push bars, so that it was easy to get out. Eventually, local fire brigades began to take responsibility for making sure the owners of theatres and cinemas obeyed these new laws.

Heritage Trail

THE GLEN CINEMA

THE GLEN CINEMA FORMED ONE SECTION OF THE GOOD TEMPLARS' BUILDING AND WAS ENTERED FROM DYERS' WYND. ON HOGMANAY 1929, IT WAS PACKED WITH CHILDREN WHEN SMOKE WAS SEEN IN THE PROJECTION ROOM. IN THE ENSUING PANIC 69 CHILDREN LOST THEIR LIVES. THEY ARE COMMEMORATED BY A MONUMENT IN HAWKHEAD CEMETERY.

Renfrew District Council

A plaque commemorating the 1929 Paisley cinema fire

Petrol was a new type of fire hazard for the fire brigades at this time. Cars, lorries, tractors and aeroplanes all used petrol in their engines, which often caught alight. Firefighters found that tipping sand onto a petrol fire starved the fire of oxygen so that it went out. You can still see buckets of sand at service stations today.

Early twentieth-century firemen in their brass helmets

Every local fire brigade had its own smart uniform. Brass helmets were often worn ... until somebody realised that, although they look smart, helmets made from brass have one big drawback – they get very hot!

Firefighters in the Second World War

In 1941, two years after the start of the Second World War, all local fire brigades were merged into one big National Fire Service. This meant that firefighters could be moved quickly from one town to another to deal more effectively with the aftermath of bomb attacks.

Night after night, enemy fighter planes dropped incendiary bombs on Britain's towns and cities. Hundreds of these bombs would be dropped at any one time. When an incendiary bomb landed it would ignite, causing a fire.

Firefighters work on a bombed building

Women! You are needed in

THE NATIONAL
FIRE SERVICE
AS FULL-TIME OR PART-TIME MEMBERS

You can train to be a telephonist, despatch rider, driver, canteen worker and for many

APPLY FOR PARTICULARS TO NEAREST FIRE STATION OR

It soon became obvious that there weren't enough full-time firefighters to cope, so all sorts of people, like teachers, shop assistants and factory workers, were encouraged to become part-time firefighters and join the Auxiliary Fire Service.

Many women joined the Auxiliary Fire Service. They became drivers or worked behind the scenes. Others worked as dispatch riders, riding motorbikes through the rubble-strewn streets with important messages for the firefighters. Some of them were as young as fourteen!

Men and women became fireguards, too. Fireguards looked out for incendiary bombs. They were issued with a bucket of sand, a bucket of water and a stirrup pump, so that they could try and put out any fire before it took hold.

Fire and rescue services today

After the Second World War, the role of firefighters began to change. They found themselves being called out to help rescue people who were trapped in floods, or who were stuck down the side of a cliff. Gradually, most fire brigades changed their names and became Fire and Rescue Services.

From the 1950s onwards, the increase in cars and lorries on Britain's roads led to a growing number of road traffic collisions. More and more, firefighters found themselves having to rescue people trapped inside crashed cars. Fire engines soon started to carry a first aid kit, metal cutters, a hacksaw and a tool box as well as hoses, ladders and water.

Firefighters attending a flooded area

Not all firefighters work full-time. Part-time or 'on-call' firefighters do everyday jobs like working in a shop or an office. But when the call comes through from the fire service control centre, they leave work and head straight out to whatever emergency they are required to attend. On-call firefighters are trained to carry out the full range of fire and rescue duties.

Firefighters learning how to deal with a road traffic collision

Today's firefighters also help rescue people who are trapped on cliffs, in quarries or underground in caves. For this they have special ladders and winches.

Firefighters can find themselves being called out to some very odd incidents, such as rescuing a horse that has fallen into a swimming pool

The Urban Search and Rescue service

A special Urban Search and Rescue service, known as the USAR service, was established in Britain in 2008. As well as being on standby for terrorist attacks, teams of USAR firefighters are also responsible for responding to major incidents such as collapsed buildings or train crashes.

There are 23 teams of USAR firefighters across England, Scotland, Wales and Northern Ireland. In each team there are thirty specially trained firefighters and a dog. The dog's job is to sniff out people who have become trapped in collapsed buildings. Since 2008, Britain's USAR teams have responded to over 1,100 incidents around the country.

A USAR sniffer dog and handler

USAR teams regularly undertake special practice exercises to learn how to deal with major events. One of these was 'Exercise Teal', when USAR teams practised dealing with a major aircraft incident for more than three days!

USAR firefighters taking part in Exercise Teal

A United Kingdom International Search and Rescue team attending an earthquake in Nepal in 2015

The United Kingdom International Search and Rescue (UK ISAR) team is on call 24 hours a day to respond to natural disasters, such as floods and earthquakes, anywhere in the world. Thirteen local fire and rescue services take it in turns to be ready and on call to respond to International Search and Rescue requests.

The control centre

Before telephones were invented, fire stations used to hear about a fire in their area from 'runners'. These were men or boys who dashed from the fire to the fire station with a message. In London they were paid one shilling (5p) for each run they made. Today, every local fire and rescue service has its own control centre.

When you dial 999, the operator asks you which service you require: fire, police or ambulance. If you ask for the fire service, your call will be put through to the local Fire and Rescue Service Control Centre. The control centre operators make sure that calls are answered quickly and that information about the incident is passed on to the nearest fire station. For major incidents, such as a large house fire or a multiple vehicle collision, they may contact more than one fire station or ask for specialist appliances, like an extendable ladder.

A fire and rescue service control centre

SHE IS FIRST TO DIAL 999

Arrest Follows

Mr. Stanley Beard, of Elsworthy-road, Hampstead, heard a noise outside his house at 4.20 a.m., and, on looking out, saw a man's foot.

His wife immediately dialled the new emergency number "999" and asked for "police." Seconds later radio patrol cars raced to the spot. Four minutes later a man was detained by the police near Primrose Hill.

Later in the day Thomas Duffy (24), labourer, was charged at Marylebone Police Court with attempting to break into the house, and was remanded in custody.

999 is the world's oldest emergency call service, having launched in 1937. Today you can also dial 112, the European emergency services number, which works in all European Union countries.

The first ever 999 call was headline news.

When the 999 service was first set up, everybody with a telephone in their house was sent a letter with these instructions on how to use it

This letter from your Telephone Manager is IMPORTANT to you as a telephone subscriber and it should be preserved

EMERGENCY CALLS FOR "FIRE", "POLICE", "AMBULANCE", DIAL "999"

Dear Sir/Madam,

A new procedure is being introduced at your exchange to enable you, by dialling to secure the special attention of the operator for calls to the Fire Service, Police or A... Authorities on occasions of emergency. For this purpose, special equipment has been installed exchange so that, when "999" is dialled, an emergency lamp and loud buzzer will indicate to operator that the call is specially urgent. The telephone numbers of the Fire, Police and Ambula... Authorities are prominently displayed for the information of the operators and... authorities will be secured by simply asking the exchange... "Ambulance!" as the case may be.

In you...

29

Fire safety advice

All local fire and rescue services have people on their teams who can advise you about fire safety.

You can ask your local fire service to send someone to visit your home so that they can advise you and your family on fire prevention. They will help you to install smoke detectors.

You might even have met firefighters at your school, giving talks about fire safety.

If you discover a fire in your building, remember: never take chances.

- *Get out*
- *Stay out!*
- *Call 999*

Firefighters regularly visit schools to give talks about fire safety

Glossary

apparatus Equipment.

dispatch rider A motorbike rider who delivers important messages.

dockyard A place alongside a river where ships and boats are unloaded.

engulfed Surrounded.

ferocity Fierceness.

firebreak A clearing made between buildings so that fire can't spread.

fireguard Someone who keeps a look out for fires that have been started by bombs.

fire mark A sign on a building that once let firemen know which company the building was insured with.

hacksaw A saw for cutting metal.

holds The storage area in the bottom of ships.

improper Unsuitable or against the rules.

incendiary bomb A bomb which, on landing, bursts into flames and starts a fire.

off-roader A special vehicle, usually with big wheels and tyres, that can be driven across fields.

runner Someone who delivers important messages on foot.

smoke detector An electronic gadget that 'beeps' loudly when it senses smoke in a room.

smouldering When something is burning, but there are no flames.

stirrup pump A hand pump.

vigiles Roman firefighters.

Index

Published in Great Britain in 2018 by Wayland

Copyright © Wayland, 2016

All rights reserved.
ISBN: 978 1 5263 0535 0
10 9 8 7 6 5 4 3 2 1

Printed in China

MIX
Paper from
responsible sources
FSC® C104740

Wayland
An imprint of
Hachette Children's Group
Part of Hodder & Stoughton
Carmelite House
50 Victoria Embankment
London EC4Y 0DZ

An Hachette UK Company
www.hachette.co.uk
www.hachettechildrens.co.uk

Author: Roy Apps
Editor: Liza Miller
Designer: Lisa Peacock
Consultant: Timothy Cross, National Archives

The National Archives is the UK government's official archive
containing over 1,000 years of history. They give detailed
guidance to government departments and the public sector on
information management, and advise others about the care of
historical archives.

Cover illustrations: Kerry Hyndman
Images © The National Archives: 2l, 3, 6, 7t, 16t, 16b, 21b, 22,
23t, 29t, 29b, 30t

Picture credits:
3r: Tim Large/Shutterstock; 4: Mary Evans Picture Library; 5t:
American Academy in Rome, Photographic Archive; 5b: Lagui/
Shutterstock; 7b: Bikeworldtravel/Shutterstock; 8: London Fire
Brigade/Mary Evans; 9: BazzaDaRambler/Wikimedia; 11b: Kim
Traynor/Wikimedia; 12: Science Museum/Science & Society
Picture Library; 13t: withGod/Shutterstock; 13b: Monkey
Business Images/Shutterstock; 14: Museum of London; 15t:
Oldham Evening Chronicle; 15b: Marilyn Barbone/Shutterstock;
17t: Manfred Gottschalk/Getty; 17b: Jack Sullivan/Alamy
Stock Photo; 18: The Mistress and Fellows, Girton College,
Cambridge; 19: Monkey Business Images/Shutterstock; 20:
SASSBS/Wikimedia; 21t: Paul Broadbent/Alamy Stock Photo;
23b: Imperial War Museum; 25t: ChiccoDodiFC/Shutterstock;
25b: DPA Picture Alliance Archive/Alamy Stock Photo; 26:
Burnstuff2003/Dreamstime; 27t: Buckinghamshire Fire &
Rescue Service; 27b: Jessica Lea/DFID; 28: Graham Taylor/
Shutterstock; 30b: ChameleonsEye/Shutterstock.